*Centering
Moments!
Volume III*

Copyright Page

Centering Moments Vol III

Dr. Darryl L Claybon

Copyright©2016

by Darryl L Claybon

All Rights Reserved

ISBN: 978-0-9862366-4-8

Printed in the United States

For Information Contact:

Dr. Darryl L. Claybon

Atlanta, GA

404-213-6313

drcitc@gmail.com

Cover design by Dr. Darryl L. Claybon

Graphics by Ms. Rhodia Hernandez

Consulting by Dr. Carolyn Carter Townsel

Acknowledgements

To God be the Glory, the Honor, and the
Praise.
Just let me live my life
And let it be pleasing, Lord to Thee
And should I gain any praise,
Let it go to Calvary. **Andrae Crouch**

To my family and friends: Thank you for all
that you have invested, given, and poured into
me. I never would have made it without you...

To my students: Thank you for the moments
when the student became the teacher and this
teacher became the student.

ἀπεκρίθη ὁ Πιλᾶτος ὃ γέγραφα γέγραφα
Pilate answered, What I have written I have
written. **John 19:22 (KJV)**

Purpose

A man is traveling through the wilderness. Tired and thirsty, he stumbles upon an old well. He franticly begins to use the handle to pump the water out of the well. However, since the well had not been used in quite a while, the pump was dry. The man sits on a well, growing even thirstier.

As he wearily looks around he sees a sign that says, "Please refill" and an arrow pointing downward. Underneath is a sealed glass jar filled with water. At first, the man's impulse is to drink the water from the jar. However, the sign said, "Please Refill." The man ponders for a moment, and then opens the jar.

He walks over to the well, pours the water from the jar into the well's pump, thus priming the pump. After a few pumps, the water begins to flow from the well. The man, before he drinks, refills the jar and replaces it under the sign that says "Please refill."

Centering moments are simply meant to be a jar of water one uses to only "prime the pump." Centering Moments are not meant to be an exhaustive exegesis of the text. The intention is a dialogue as opposed to a monologue.

Foreword

Often we wonder where to begin a new year, a new month, a new day, a new job, a new or current marriage, or a new relationship.

We also wonder where to begin during the difficult times as well as in the aftermath of pain, sickness, the loss of a loved one, a broken relationship, divorce, family crisis, financial ruin or just some very bad decisions.

Whether the times are good or bad, there is always a place to start. Centering Moments Volume IV provides four key lessons in utilizing the Biblical principles of "Sitting" provided by Jesus in his Judean teaching ministry.

The lessons are designed to enrich one's critical thinking skills by using real time life applications. The stories are by no means exhaustive, but intended to start the conversation. The reader will find there are more questions than answers. However, the goal is to stir up the gifts within, and create a thirst and love for more knowledge of our Lord.

Sitting before Starting helps us to understand where to start. *Sitting before Serving* helps us understand how to start. *Sitting before Sending* helps us develop the team around us as we start. *Sitting while being Served* teaches us to value and organize our resources while continuing the practice of sitting after we start.

Love, Peace & Blessings,

Darryl

Table of Contents

Centering Moment I

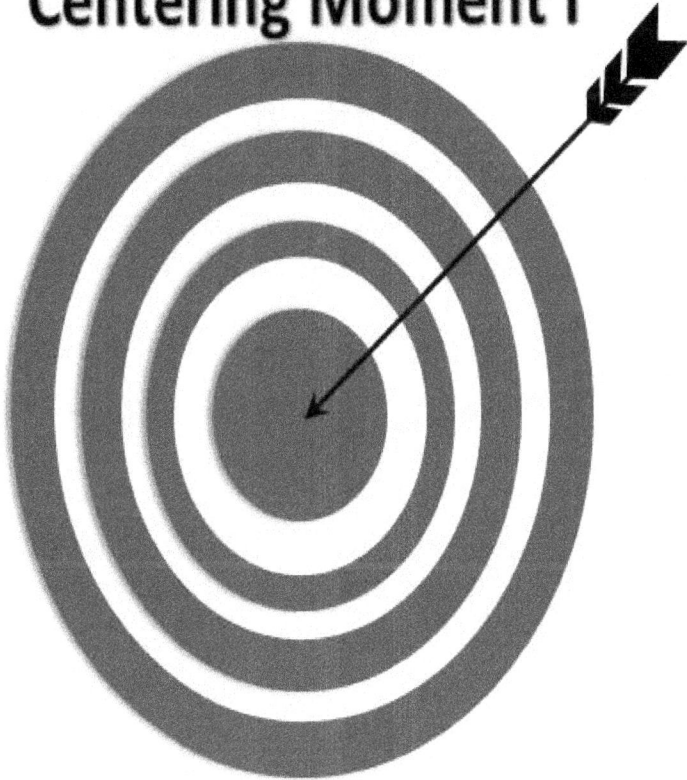

Case Study 1

James is feeling frustrated with his current job. He does not like the hours nor does he like the salary. James does not like the boss or the other employees. He hates having to catch the train at 5:00 A.M every morning and longs for the day when he can afford a car.

At lunch, he sits down with his co-worker Ann that he is not going to return to work. He declares "I quit!"

Ann listens to James' concerns. She wants James to think about the consequences of leaving his job in this manner.

Questions:

If James is not happy, should he quit his job?

Is Ann right, suggesting that leaving in this manner is not appropriate? What are the consequences?

What are some suggestions Ann can make?

Centering Moment I

LUKE 14

28 For which of you, intending to build a tower, does not first sit down and estimate the cost, to see whether he has enough to complete it? 29 Otherwise, when he has laid a foundation and is not able to finish, all who see it will begin to ridicule him, 30 saying, 'This fellow began to build and was not able to finish.'

Sitting Before Starting

Finish what you start!

Setting

In our story, we find a man who is building a tower. He is constructing, assembling, engineering and putting together a tower. The word tower means a fortified structure rising to a considerable height.

There are some things we do not know about this man. We do not know his name. We are not aware of the nature of his family. We do not know how tall he is, or how much he weighs. We cannot determine his age, and there is no indication of his level of experience or expertise.

We do not know much about the tower. How tall is the tower being built? How wide is this tower? What kind of material is he using? Is the tower at the edge of the city, or in the northern region? Is the tower able to withstand hurricane winds or torrential rains?

Further, we do not know the purpose of this tower. Is the tower for personal or communal benefit? After building the tower, who will be the watchman?

It is not clear why this man is building this tower. In the Judean culture, People erected towers for one of two reasons: First, to repel a hostile attack or second, to enable a watchman to see in every direction.

There is little doubt such towers are needful today. It would be wonderful to have a watchman in a tower that can see in every direction. The watchman upon seeing the enemy or trouble coming could send us a text or tweet saying that trouble is on its way to our house. We need that kind of tower today.

Again, while Luke does not give a particular reason for the building of the tower, neither are there any details regarding height, width, or breadth, nor the types of materials assembled. One may reason for this omission is the first-century reader is very familiar with the process and procedures for such a project.

Jesus' audience no doubt understands what it takes to build a tower.

There is also one more item of interest. Why is this man working alone? Where are the other workers? Here, in the twenty-first century, we understand the perils of building alone. One can burn out quickly when one is doing all of the work alone. Not many things are accomplished alone. It is even written, "It is not good for the man to be alone!" One may argue here as well; the first-century reader has a familiarity with tower building that we do not have access. For us, this appears to be a very lonely project: perhaps, even doomed from the start.

Situation

However, the problem Jesus has with this man is not that he is starting to build a tower. Jesus is not concerned with the height, depth, nor breathe of the tower. It even appears that even if the man is building alone, it seems to be the least of Jesus' concerns. Jesus's problem is not that the man started building the tower, but the problem is the man's inability to finish what he started.

Jesus seizes the moment by offering " which of you, intending to build a tower, will not sit down, and estimate the cost, to see if he has enough to complete it. The least you can do is sit down and estimate, approximate, guess, and get what is called a ballpark figure before starting.

This man's inability to finish is intensified further when he has laid the foundation. Jesus says, "After laying the foundation, and is not able to finish, then all who see it, began to ridicule and mock him!"(NRSV)Saying this man is not able to finish. (NRSV)

In other words, they put him on Facebook. They text, tweet, and Instagram him and put him on blast because he cannot finish. One cannot help but wonder, what is this man's problem? Why would he just start building and not consider the cost?

One can easily be a little upset with the man until one starts thinking about the reasons, he may have stopped building. There are quite a few reasons that a person will halt the building process. There could be geographical, political, and economic reasons that bring the project to a halt.

Perhaps the man is stressed by the systemic "isms" of his day. People, family and friends can slow down the process significantly. Also, sickness can disrupt the best laid plans. The sickness of a loved one or the loss of a loved one will bring any project or plan to a grinding halt.

However, while these may be perfect and legitimate reasons not to finish, Jesus point is well taken; the man did not sit down and count up the cost!

Solution

However, there is some good news in the text.

1 He has a Vision

28 For which of you, intending to build a tower,

First, the man building the tower has a vision and a desire to build a tower. There are many people today that have neither a vision nor desire to do a thing. They sit on their hands all day long complaining and making fun of the workers that are doing something.

Jesus said "those that see him begin to mock him, but one can only wonder what those people were doing. It would seem the appropriate thing for the mocking people to do is either help the man or ask the man that is building the tower for a job.

2 He Starts Building

30 saying, "This fellow began to build"

Second, not only does the man have a vision and a desire to build, he actually starts building. Some people are still waiting for the perfect conditions to build. This man understands that there are no perfect conditions and begins to build in spite of the environment. He may not have all that he needs, but he still begins to build.

He may have even started knowing I cannot finish, but my record in heaven will show, that I did get started. He may have been operating under the presumption that if I build it, they will come.

The world would be a better place if folks would adjourn the councils of procrastinators, waiters, and haters, and call to order the meeting of the devoted, the determined and the dedicated and begin building while singing the old Negro spiritual "If I had a hammer, I would hammer in the morning, I would hammer in the evening, all over this land."

3 He Lays a Foundation

29 Otherwise, when he has laid a foundation

Third, the man does lay a foundation. Some credit is due to this man. Persons that lay foundations are critical, crucial, and imperative.

1 Corinthians 3:11

For no one can lay any foundation other than the one that has been laid; that foundation is Jesus Christ. (NRSV)

Grandmothers and Grandfathers who never went to school a day in their lives laid the foundation so their children could graduate from college. Hard working men and women built and paid for schools brick by brick, bake sale by bake sale. Those same brave men and women never asked for anything in return, not even so much as their name on the cornerstone. They only wanted to see their children graduate from college!

Before a skyscraper is started, a company has to come in and lay a foundation. The building may be beautiful, elegant, and pristine against the skyline of a major international city, but let the record reflect that no matter how tall it stands, it sits on a foundation that someone laid: The taller the building, the deeper the foundation.

Conclusion

A wise person once said that failure to plan is indeed a plan to fail. Also, it is written, "that if you do not have a plan, people will make plans for you."

According to Jesus, this gentleman's failure appears to start at the beginning. It is a project that is doomed from the start simply because he did not sit down before starting up. As you plan your New Year, new month, new week, new project, new plan, new idea, new job, new marriage, new relationship, or new day, please be encouraged to please sit down and count up the cost before starting. *Selah!*

Questions:

1 Who gives us our dreams and visions?

2 Are some dreams and visions too big?

3 Are there always going to be perfect conditions to start a project?

4 Is it okay to try to do something and fail?

5 What is your vision and have you started?

Notes

Centering Moment II

Case Study II

James gets a new job. He is ecstatic! He likes the hours, and he loves the salary. James enjoys his new boss and the other employees. Because of the increase in pay, he is able to afford a new car.

He decides not to sit down with the New Employee Orientation committee. He declares "I already know how to do this job!"

However, the new company has some different equipment and computers that James is not used to operating. On his first day, James makes a lot of mistakes and costs the company a lot of money. The manager is outraged with James.

Questions:

What is the purpose of the New Employee Orientation?

Should James have gone to the New Employee Orientation? What are the consequences of not going?

Should the manager sit down with James and explain why James cost the company a lot of money or just terminate him?

Sitting Before Serving

Everything you need,

is not in the Kitchen!

Luke 10:38-42 (NRSV)

[38] Now as they went on their way, he entered a certain village, where a woman named Martha welcomed him into her home. [39] She had a sister named Mary, who sat at the Lord's feet and listened to what he was saying. [40] But Martha was distracted by her many tasks; so she came to him and asked, "Lord, do you not care that my sister has left me to do all the work by myself? Tell her then to help me." [41] But the Lord answered her, "Martha, Martha, you are worried and distracted by many things; [42] there is need of only one thing. Mary has chosen the better part, which will not be taken away from her."

Setting

In our story, Jesus is in the home of Martha and Mary. Martha and Mary are the sisters of Lazarus. Recall when Lazarus became ill, it was Martha and Mary that sent word saying "Lazarus the one whom you love is sick!"

Jesus is in the home. Luke says "She opens her home to him." The sisters provide something that is indeed missing in many societies today. They provide good ole fashioned hospitality.

We are not sure if Jesus is tired, hungry, and exhausted, but we are confident that if Jesus is, He welcomes their warmth, kindness, and generosity. Jesus responds by entering into their home. Perhaps some of the most powerful words spoken since the beginning of time: Jesus is in the home! The world would be a better place if Jesus could spend more time in our homes.

Also note, that the sisters provide two types of hospitality. There is what is called sitting hospitality, and then there is serving hospitality.

Jesus and Mary are in the family room; Mary sits at the feet of Jesus. That is to say; she is retaining the posture of a student in the presence of the teacher. Mary listens to what he is saying. She is a hearer of the word.

Neither scholars nor theologians know what lessons Jesus the Great Teacher is sharing. Some believe He may be sharing some deep theological secret of the foundations of the world. Since Jesus was there when God says "Let there be light!" He may be sharing some thoughts about what God was doing before God stepped out of nowhere, and created somewhere. Jesus may have answered the

Psalmist who wrote in Psalms 8 "What is man that thou are mindful of him?"

We would love to know what He shares with Mary. Perhaps Jesus simply tells Mary to hold on a little while longer, because everything is going to be alright after a while. Maybe He shares that God is a way-maker and can make a way out of no way! Perhaps He reminds her "Mary don't you weep, and tell Martha not to mourn, for Pharaoh's army drowned in the Red sea! That would be "Reed Sea" for the Bible scholars.

Mary has probably lost her student posture by this time. She is dancing and shouting all over the family room. Saying "I wasn't gonna tell nobody, but I just could not keep to myself!" Let the record show, the world would be a better place, if folk dance and shouted at home like they do at church!

Dance and shout at those times when things are not going well! At those times when the husband is not sticking with the plan, the wife is not sticking with the budget, and the kids are not sticking to anything. That's a reason to sing, dance, and shout!

Situation

But while Mary is celebrating and rejoicing in the family room, Martha is in the kitchen working up a sweat. Martha takes her long flowing hair and puts it in a ball. She places a long hairpin in it to keep the heat coming from the hair off her neck.

Perspiration is pouring from her forehead and lapping under her chin. She uses the bottom of her apron to desperately wipe the moisture away and keep the huge beads of sweat from dripping into her eyes. However, because it is hot in the kitchen, the sweat and the heat cause her eyes to sting, burn, and turn red.

Something about hair lying on the back of the neck produces a temperature that cannot be easily sustained by mortal man or woman. The kitchen is hot with heat that is comparable to the fire pits of Hell: an agonizing and eternal fire!

Hearing her sister rejoicing in the living room does not add to Martha's joy. Not only are Martha's eyes stinging, burning, and red, but her anger has reached the boiling point.

Just a reminder, in case you are not aware, but everybody is not happy when you are shouting. At this juncture, Martha is what we call "pistol hot!" Pistol hot is when one is angry and hot at the same time! Martha flies out of the kitchen and into the family room. Jesus and Mary are about to find out that their little joyful centering moment has come to an end.

Martha speaks using the fullness of her earthiness. Rest assured she is not speaking in a spiritual tone. But with the wrath of a contentious woman who is scorned: "Don't you care?" Many of us find ourselves echoing those thoughts and words: "Really Jesus?" Is this what it has come down too?

"Don't you care that my sister has left me to do the work myself?" You and this dear sister of mine are in here laughing and having fun and I'm strung out in this hot @#$ kitchen. Martha is careful not to accuse Jesus of not helping either. However, she does vehemently suggest that the least Jesus can do is to tell Mary to help out a little bit. Martha is simply asking "do I have to cook, set the table, serve the food, and clean up?"

Telling her to help me is an earnest cry that many of us make from time to time. All of us at some point feel overwhelmed by our circumstances and the need for help. This feeling intensifies when it appears that others are not contributing to their fair share of the work.

Jesus response is a bit puzzling and even perplexing. He begins by comforting her by saying, "Martha, Martha." In some cultures to say someone's name twice is a sign of endearment. "You are worried and upset about many things. But few things are needed, indeed only one. Mary has chosen the good part that shall not be taken from her."

"What did he just say?" is probably what Martha is thinking. What has that to do with it being hot in the kitchen? What has that to do with this dear little sister of mine, not lifting a finger to help her overworked sister? Why is Mary allowed to sit and not help?

Final questions, why did Jesus not do the miracle thing? He turned water into wine; cannot he turn water into dishwater? Did Mary have to do any cooking at all? More importantly, why does Jesus, the non-conforming, non-traditionalist, not help Martha?

Solution

Sitting

39 She had a sister named Mary, who sat at the Lord's feet and listened to what he was saying.

First, this story suggests that Mary knows that everything she needs "is not in the kitchen!" Mary is a forward thinker. She is not relying on a standing tradition in a changing world. Her mission is to serve this present age, and the tradition of holding down the kitchen is not her   only   opportunity.

In many instances, the church talks about church growth, but the church growth is on the church's terms. The church wants to recruit people who look like us, walk like us, and talk like us. Mary decides there is more to life than just the traditional role.

Serving

⁴⁰ But Martha was distracted by her many tasks;

Second, Jesus never calls Martha out of the kitchen. Again, this is mystifying and perplexing. Jesus knows of Martha's dilemma, yet Jesus does not assist her.

28 "Come to me, all you that are weary and are carrying heavy burdens and I will give you rest. 29 Take my yoke upon you, and learn from me; for I am gentle and humble in heart, and you will find rest for your souls. Matthew 11:28-29 (NRSV)

Now it seems that Jesus is saying "Martha you are worried about the wrong thing." You need to stay in your lane. Many things are necessary, but it comes down to one thing. Ensure that you have a relationship with Jesus. Mary has chosen the good part. Many find fulfillment in sitting first. Mary sits before serving.

Hearers and Doers

41 But the Lord answered her, "Martha, Martha, you are worried and distracted by many things; 42 there is need of only one thing. Mary has chosen the better part, which will not be taken away from her."

Finally, this story suggests that Mary is a hearer of the word, but Martha is a doer of the word!

Notice, Jesus did not call Martha out of the kitchen, but at the same time, Jesus did not send Martha back to the kitchen. Martha can step out of the tradition and into the present age when ready. The story suggests that the only persons holding us in our traditional role are ourselves! You may step out at any time!

Conclusion

The two sisters represent the dichotomy within all of us. We fully understand the importance of serving. Martha lives out the creed of "loving others as we love ourselves. She demonstrates her love through serving others. Mary, on the other hand, represents that part of us that needs to sit in the presence of Jesus, before serving. The longer we sit, the better we can serve.

Questions:

1 Did Martha need help in the kitchen?

2 Should Mary help in the kitchen?

3 Should Martha have to ask for help?

4 What is the good part that Mary has chosen?

5 Which area of your life or home do you need the most help?

Notes

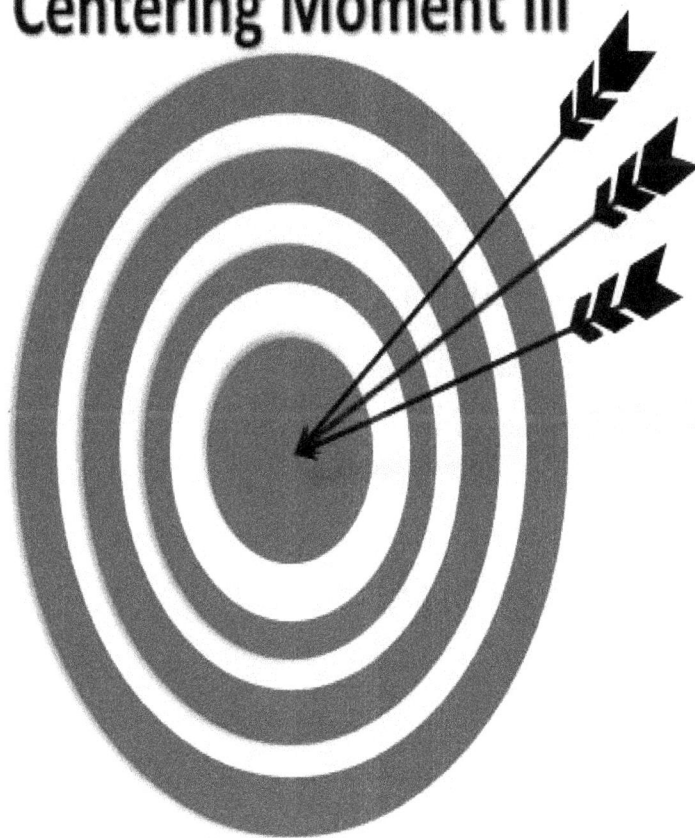

Centering Moment III

Case Study III

Joan has to send out emails to 1700 employees. The emails contain instructions for the employees to enroll in the insurance program for the next year.

She procrastinates and sends the emails during the last week of enrollment. Also, because she does it at the last minute, she does not sit down and let someone else proofread the email with her.

The emails have the current year's enrollment link. The employees click the link and receive a message saying they are already enrolled. Needless to say, now 1700 employees will not have insurance for the following year.

Questions:

Is Joan in trouble?

What can happen when a person procrastinates?

Should she have let someone else proofread the email before sending it?

Centering Moment III
Sitting Before Sending

"You have to know when to fold em"

Luke 14

[31] Or what king, going out to wage war against another king, will not sit down first and consider whether he is able with ten thousand to oppose the one who comes against him with twenty thousand? [32] If he cannot, then, while the other is still far away, he sends a delegation and asks for the terms of peace.

Setting

In our story, we find a king that is about to fight a war that he cannot win. The war is over before it begins. Our culture defines war as a state of armed conflict between different nations or states or different groups within a nation or state. We are not sure if the war is between nations or states. We are not certain if the conflict is between groups within a nation or state such as a civil war. Wars between nations are often uneasy propositions but can be necessary and just. Wars within nations or states appear to be a little more atrocious when brothers fight against brothers.

The particular reasons for this war are not certain. We do know that blood and treasure are the top priorities and at the highest risk. In war, there is the possibility that both stand the chance of being lost. The king, the leader of the nation, must assume the responsibility of assuring mothers and fathers that the soldiers, their sons, and daughters, have the opportunity for a safe return.

Situation

However, for this particular king, this king is about to engage in a war that he cannot win. He is fighting a losing battle. He has the necessary information to make a calculated, efficient, and effective decision. He is going to lose the war.

Someone here today, may not only feel they are fighting a losing battle but know in their heart of hearts, that it is time to wave the white flag of surrender. Someone is saying, "I have exhausted all of my resources. I have all of the information I need to render a decision, and it appears this battle is over before it begins."

It seems that Jesus is not necessarily disturbed that this king is going to lose. Jesus is not distressed about the king's leadership skills. He appears to be a capable leader, for there is no indication that the soldiers will not follow him into battle. The king's men give the impression they are prepared. There is no evidence the men are not ready for combat. There is no indication that the king or the nation has violated a holy covenant and the Lord is no longer on their side. The only problem Jesus is having with this king is that this king and the king's army are outnumbered!

It is true that smaller armies have beaten larger armies. But Jesus seizes the moment by saying:

"What king, going out to wage war against another king, will not sit down first and consider whether he is able with ten thousand to oppose the one who comes against him with twenty thousand?"

Jesus is offering that if a king is outnumbered, the first thing a king or queen, needs to do is sit down! That is the first step. Then consider whether he is able with ten thousand soldiers, can overcome a king that has twenty thousand soldiers. Jesus is not saying that it is impossible, but please engage in some critical thinking before starting the war.

In critical thinking, one sits down and considers all of the outcomes in a given situation. One sits down, defines the problem, and lists the possible solutions along with the pros and cons of each solution. Then one can effectively make a decision.

Jesus is not saying to the king do not fight the war! Jesus is saying before you go to war, consider all of the outcomes. One may want to win, and one may want the victory, but has one counted up the cost of this victory?

Solution:

After examining the king's state of affairs, Jesus utters three heartbreaking words: "If he cannot!" It simply means that the king is about to engage in a no-win situation. The king is about to fight a war that he cannot possibly win.

Then Jesus proposes, advises, and highly recommends three things that speak to us today and advances the notion of the importance of critical thinking and preparation:

First: Develop a winning timeline!
Luke 14: 32 If he cannot, then, while the other is still far away,

While the other is still far away, the king with ten thousand soldiers starts thinking forward. He creates a schedule and sticks to it. He is up early while others are sleeping. He understands if he starts now, while the other king is at a great distance, there is the more likelihood that a deal can be worked out. The losing king understands that procrastination will not serve any purpose. Seize the moment! Make the first step now! Do not put off for tomorrow what you can do today.

Second: Develop a winning team!

Luke 14: 32(b) he sends a delegation,

He sends a delegation. The losing king also understands the importance of forming alliances and partnerships. He realizes that he needs people that are skilled in the art of negotiating. He needs teammates that can represent him in every capacity. A team that is so entrenched in this king's vision, that when the king that has twenty thousand speaks to the delegation, it is as though he is speaking to the king of the ten thousand personally.

Third: Develop winning tactics and strategies

Luke 14: 32 (c) he sends a delegation and asks for the terms of peace.

Ask for terms of peace. The losing king becomes a winning king when he is able to develop a strategy, plan, and policy, in which all parties can agree. Jesus deems terms of peace as the optional approach.

One should continue to develop strategies that de-escalate conflict, confusion and promotes clarity. The losing king's position is of a very delicate nature, and the goal is to preserve both blood and treasure!

Conclusion:

"Every battle is won before it's ever fought."
— Sun Tzu

Someone today, may not only feel they are fighting a losing battle but know in their heart of hearts, that it is time to wave the white flag of surrender. Someone is saying, I have exhausted all of my resources. I have all of the information I need to render a decision, and it appears this war is over before it begins. But remember, there is time to negotiate terms of peace so that losses are minimized and relationships are maximized. Therefore, be not dismayed, neither be afraid, God will take care of you!

Questions:

1 What does it mean to be outnumbered?

2 Did the losing king have any other alternatives?

3 How important is it to develop a winning schedule every day?

4 How important is it that your teammates understand your values and goals?

5 What are some of your winning tactics and strategies?

Notes

Centering Moment IV

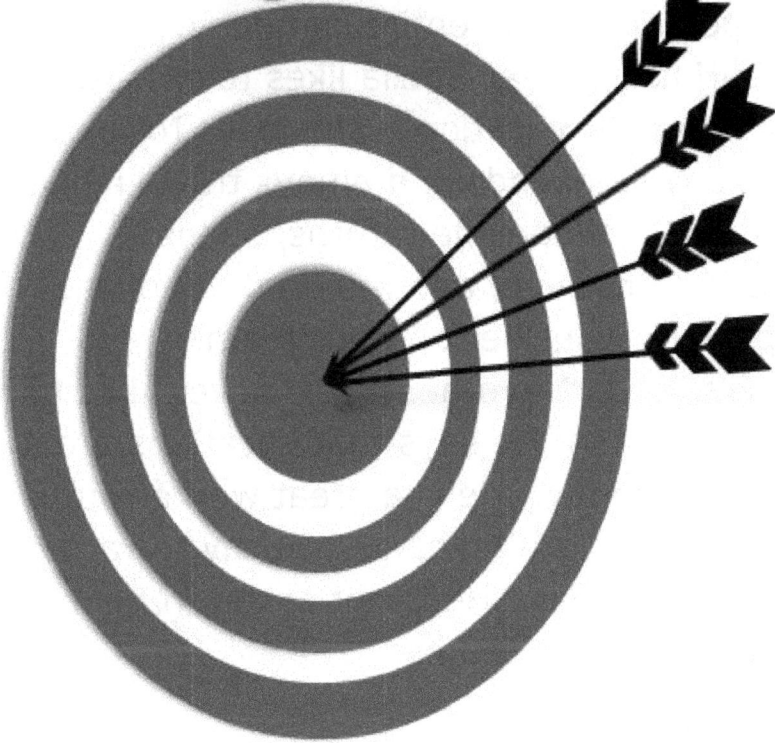

Case Study IV

Frank and Shelia are the top performing salespersons in the entire company.

During the year Shelia likes to sit down and plan mini-vacations. She loves to take three day weekends and enjoys traveling with her family. When she returns, she is refreshed, revived, and restored. All of the employees want her on their team.

Frank, on the other hand, never likes to go on vacation. He says that vacations are a waste of money. He is a great worker but is often moody, grumpy and grouchy toward the other employees. He is not asked frequently to work on other teams.

Questions:

Can an employee be moody, grumpy, and grouchy, and still be a top performing salesperson?

Is it okay to sit down, plan, and take a mini-vacation every once in a while? What are the benefits?

What happens if a person works all of the time?

Centering Moment IV

Sitting While Being Served

John 6

5 When he looked up and saw a large crowd coming toward him, Jesus said to Philip, "Where are we to buy bread for these people to eat?" **6** He said this to test him, for he himself knew what he was going to do. **7** Philip answered him, "Six months' wages[b] would not buy enough bread for each of them to get a little." **8** One of his disciples, Andrew, Simon Peter's brother, said to him, **9** "There is a boy here who has five barley loaves and two fish. But what are they among so many people?" **10** Jesus said, "Make the people sit down." Now there was a great deal of grass in the place; so they[c] sat down, about five thousand in all. **11** Then Jesus took the loaves, and when he had given thanks, he distributed them to those who were seated; so also the fish, as much as they wanted.

Setting

In our story, Jesus is being followed by large crowds. The crowds have heard of the sick people that were healed by Jesus. Therefore, no matter where Jesus traveled, people managed to find him.

People would spread the word that Jesus was in a certain place, and everyone would stop what they were doing, and rush to the broadcasted location. The world would be an incredible place if more people would seek and find Jesus.

These first-century crowds put Jesus on the equivalent of Facebook, Twitter, Instagram, Snapchat, emails and texts. Someone reading this will say they did not have this kind of technology in the Bible days. That is true, but they did have Christ-Based Communications called C.B. radios, Angels, better known as sky pagers, Wireless communication by way of the

Holy Spirit, and Jesus' Grapevine which we call today "by word of mouth."

Jesus and Truckers

Jesus: Breaker, Breaker one-nine, Jesus is on the mainline!

Trucker: What is your ten-twenty J. C. (ten-twenty means location)

Jesus: I'm up here around mile marker 213 headed up the King's highway.

Trucker: What's yer ETA?

Jesus: I am always on time!

Trucker: Ten-four there good buddy, I'm east bound and down!

Situation:

John, the writer of the texts, says when Jesus looks up he sees a large crowd coming toward him. Jesus' immediate discernment of the large crowd is the crowd's need for food.

The critical thinking process begins with defining the problem. One can presume they had other needs but the paramount need ascertained by Jesus is the crowd is hungry. Jesus understands it is hard to minister to the soul when the body is crying out for physical sustenance.

"Where are we to buy bread for these people to eat?" 6 He said this to test him, for he himself knew what he was going to do. 7 Philip answered him, "Six months' wages would not buy enough bread for each of them to get a little."

Since He has established the most pressing problem at this moment, Jesus says to Phillip, where can we buy bread for these people to eat? Jesus identifies the problem and immediately begins to brainstorm regarding possible solutions. Notice that Jesus also includes his team in the brainstorming process. A good leader will be the first to try and solve the problem, but a great leader will involve the team in the problem-solving process.

He specifically asks Phillip this question. There is some speculation about Phillip living in the region and may have some familiarity with the local resources. However, Phillip's answer is a bit disconcerting. Phillips's concern is not "where" to buy bread, but his concern is "how" we are going to buy bread.

Even though that was not the question, Jesus asked, it did allow the reader to see the anxiety associated with Jesus's affinity, fixation, and desire to feed this crowd.

Phillip's focus was on the cost. Phillip says "Six months' wages would not buy enough bread for each of them to get a little." Phillip is pointing out that even if we did have six months of wages, they still would only get a little. It would not be enough to satisfy the large crowd, and we will be right back where we started. Recently, a church person was overheard saying "We don't have that kind of money for this type of ministry!"

8 One of his disciples, Andrew, Simon Peter's brother, said to him, 9 "There is a boy here who has five barley loaves and two fish. But what are they among so many people?"

To further exasperate the situation developing, Andrew manages to find a boy with a lunch that consisted of five barley loaves and two fish. But Andrew's understanding of the resources found sounds futile, useless, and a big waste of time. Andrew questions the blessing he is holding in his hand by asking "But what are they among so many?"

Is Andrew correct? The resources seem so meager in comparison to the problem.

How can one be expected to perform in times of recession and want, as though one is operating in times of a robust, healthy, and booming economy?

Solution

So how does this first-century story speak to us today in the twenty-first century?

Regarding the critical thinking process, Jesus has identified the most pressing problem. The crowd needs healing, but more importantly they are hungry. Next, Jesus involves his team in the brainstorming process. He involves them in the beginning, so there will be little-to-no resistance securing their buy-in during the implementation stage of the critical thinking process.

First, Jesus understands His resources.
[6]He said this to test him, for he himself knew what he was going to do.

Jesus understands his resources. He knows

that the resources are limited. In Jesus's mind, the idea of ordering carry-out from a nearby establishment was not a viable option. If that were an option, then Jesus would have asked a different question: "Who is going to call and order the food?"

Phillip helps us understand, that if there is a nearby establishment, there are not enough funds in the account to purchase food. Andrew helps us understand; we do have some resources, but they are indeed limited. We may have scarce resources when we started, but our limited resources are not restricted.

Our first goal should be to seek to understand our resources. Before Jesus does anything, He organizes Himself. He plans his day. Jesus is clear about his mission today. He knows exactly how many persons He will serve and in what order they will take place. Often we start the day without organizing ourselves and our resources.

Second, Jesus Organizes His Resources.
10 Jesus said "Make the people sit down." Now there was a great deal of grass in the place; so they sat down, about five thousand in all.

Secondly, He organizes his resources by first organizing the disciples. He allows the disciples to use their skills and create order out of chaos. Jesus says to the disciples "Make the people sit down." He uses the people on his team to take care of these important details. He trusts them to do it.

Again, the clarity of the mission is handed down to the disciples. Jesus uses his leadership communication skills to ensure that each disciple is aware of the immediate goal: Time for the people to sit down! The disciples can complete their part of the assignment because their instructions are crystal clear.

Notice the disciples are not questioning or beleaguering the task. They are willing to be a part of the solution because they were a part

of the process from the beginning. The
disciples make all of the people sit down in
this grassy area.

Also, notice the area in which the crowd is
sitting is not barren, dry, or brittle. It's a place
of comfort to sit for a while and receive the
blessing. The people in need are not made to
feel small because of their circumstances.

Third, Jesus Distributes His Resources
11 Then Jesus took the loaves, and when he had
given thanks, he distributed them to those who
were seated; so also the fish, as much as they
wanted.

Jesus organizes himself and the disciples,
now the men are organized and in a position
to receive a blessing. Jesus takes the bread,
gives thanks, and distributes to those that are
seated. Also the fish is dispersed and they eat
as much as they want. Jesus asks the men to
sit and he serves them.

In our hectic world, everyone is busy doing many marvelous things. However, this story suggests that we must continue to engage in the practice of sitting. Jesus distributes his resources to "those who were seated."

The key to our success as we begin or continue our journey is to ensure that we preserve, promote, and persist in the practice of sitting down first. In doing this, we can receive the resources that only Jesus can give.

Questions:

1 Do the people in the crowd need healing or do they need food?

2 Why did Phillip start talking about cash requirements, when Jesus asked about food facilities?

3 Did Jesus view the two fish and five barley loaves as inadequate?

4 In organizing the resources, does Jesus do an excellent job ensuring that his team knows what to do?

5 As you are starting or continuing your journey, what are some ways that you can spend time sitting and receiving the resources and blessings that Jesus can give?

Notes

Bibliography/References

Cahill, Lisa Sowle. *Families: A Christian Social Perspective.* Minneapolis, MN: Fortress Press, 2000..

Carr, J. (n.d) Pouring Water on a Drowning Man. Retrieved from http://www.lyricsmode.com/lyrics/j/james_carr/pouring_water_on_a_drowning_man.html#!

Chance, J. Bradley. "Luke 15: Seeking the Outsiders." *Review & Expositor* (Spring 1994).

Chimmarusti, Rocco A. and Jay Lappin. "Beginning Family Therapy." *Family Therapy Collections,* no. 14 (1985)..

Claybon, *Darryl, L. Lessons from the Jericho Road.* (2011). Dante Publishing. Atlanta, GA

Cook, S (n.d.) Sam Cook: A change is gonna come! Retrieved from http: http://www.songfacts.com/detail.php?id=3673

Crouch, Andre. *To God be the Glory.*(1971) Retrieved from

http://www.allthelyrics.com/lyrics/andrae
_crouch/to_god_be_the_glory-lyrics-3

Dash, Michael I.N., Jonathan Jackson, and
    Stephen C. Rasor. *Hidden Wholeness: An
    African American Spirituality for
    Individuals and Communities.* Cleveland,
    OH: United Church Press, 1997.

Erickson, E. H. *Childhood and Society.* New
    York: Norton, 1950.

Farrugia, David. "Selfishness, Greed, and
    Counseling." In *Counseling & Values,*
    vol. 46 (January 2002).

Foss, Mike, and Terri Elton. *What Really
    Matters: 30 Devotions for Church
    Leadership Teams.* Loveland, CO: Group
    Publishing, 2003.

Felluga, Dino. "Modules on Freud: On
    Psychosexual Development, 1885"
    Introductory Guide to Critical Theory.
    (Purdue University) Retrieved from
    http://www.purdue.edu/guidetotheory/ps
    ychoanalysis/freud.html;

Gaye, Marvin. (1971) Inner City Blues (Make
    Me Want to Holler) Retrieved from:
hhttp://www.songfacts.com/detail.php?id=105
03

Grand Master Flash. (1982)The Message. Retrieved from http://www.metrolyrics.com/the-message-lyrics-grandmaster-flash.html

Greek Lexicon :: G2852 (KJV). Retrieved from http://www.blueletterbible.org/lang/lexicon/lexicon.cfm?Strongs=G2852&t=KJV

Hedgy, James. "Look in the Lost and Found." *Family & Life,* no. 185 (2001).

Hedrick, Charles W. "Prolegomena to Reading Parables: Luke 13: 6-9 as a Test Case." *Review and Expositor,* no. 94 (1997).

Hill, ZZ, LaSalle, Denise. Steppin out, Steppin in. (1995) Retrieved from: http://www.cduniverse.com/search/xx/music/pid/1062935/

Hidden Wholeness: An African American Spirituality for Individuals and Communities. 1997 Cleveland, OH: United Church Press

Jackson, Thomas, ed. *The Works of the Rev. John Wesley,* 14 vols. (1831) reprint, Grand Rapids, MI: Baker, 1979.

King, Albert. (1967) Down Don't Bother Me.
    Retrieved from
http://www.metrolyrics.com/down-
        don-t- bother-me-lyrics-albert-
        king.html

Lao-tzu, *The Way of Lao-tzu Chinese
    philosopher (60 BC - 531 BC.(* 2003) C
    Penguin Group (USA) Retrieved from:
http://www.quotationspage.com/quotes/Lao-
tzu

Lawrence, Tracy. (2013) Getting Used to the
    Pain. Retrieved from:
http://www.cowboylyrics.com/lyrics/lawrence-
    tracy/used-to-the-pain-16158.html

Kreeft, Peter/ Dougherty, Trent, *Socratic
    Logic. (2010)*St Augustine Pr Inc, South
    Bend, IN.

Matthew Henry, Commentary, Vol. 5, McLean,
    VA: MacDonald Publishing Company,
    1996.

Mish, Frederick C. ed. *Merriam-Webster's
    Collegiate Dictionary*, 10th ed. Springfield,
    MA: Merriam-Webster, Incorporated,
    2002.

Robertson, Anita. *Learning While Leading:
    Increasing Your Effectiveness In Ministry.*
    New York, NY:The Alban Institute, 2000.

Rothauge, Arlin J. *The Life Cycle in Congregations: A Process of Natural Creation and an Opportunity for a New Creation*. Retrieved from http://www.ecusa.anglican.org/documents/life-cycle.pdf, Internet.

Schleiermacher, Friedrich D. E. *Absolute Dependence.* 1821: English translation of 2nd ed Retrieved from http://people.bu.edu/wwildman/WeirdWil dWeb/courses/mwt/dictionary/methemes; Internet.

Slick, Mat, (n.d.) 2014 Are there apostles for today? Christian Apologetics and Research Ministry. Retrieved from: http://carm.org/

The Christian Faith. H.R. Mackintosh and J.S. Stewart, eds. London: T & T Clark, 1999.

Smith, Alanzo H., and June Smith. "Parishioner Attitudes Toward the Divorced/Separated: Awareness Seminars as Counseling Interventions." In *Counseling & Values,* no. 45 (October 2000).

Vassiliou, George A. "Analogic Communications as a Means of Joining the Family System in Therapy." *International Journal of Family Psychiatry*, no. 4 (2003).

Williams, Colin W. *John Wesley's Theology Today*. Nashville, TN: Abingdon Press, 1960.

William, M. (n.d). Mysterious apostle and his legacy, not
  easily defined. *Washington Times, The*

  (DC).

Williams, Roger and David C. Ruesink. "The Changing Rural Family ... and Community: Implications for Congregational Ministry." In *Family Ministry* (Winter 1998).

Witski, Steve. "A Preliminary Defense of Prevenient Grace" In *The Arminian Magazine*, vol. 18 no. 2 (Fall, 2000); Retrieved from: http://www.fwponline.cc/v18n2witzki.html;

Wommack, A. (2015) Paul's Thorn in the Flesh. Retrieved from: http://www.awmi.net/extra/article/paulsthorn

www.ingramcontent.com/pod-product-compliance
Lightning Source LLC
Chambersburg PA
CBHW072210090426
42740CB00012B/2466